Puppy Training:

Proven Guide to Housebreak Your Puppy in Just 7 Days

how to train your new dog in simple steps for obedience, potty training, sleep, crate training, house breaking, and dog tricks

By: Howard Hampton

Puppy Training – By Howard Hampton

Legal notice

Table of Contents

Introduction

Congratulations on your new family member! Welcoming a new puppy into your home is exciting and exhausting; having a new puppy is like having a new born baby, your puppy is going to need a lot of support, care, and supervision in the first several months in order to ensure proper behavior when he or she is older. Beginning training when puppies are younger helps to instill good habits for both you and your puppy right away. Playful biting from your puppy may be cute now, but if you don't teach puppy that hands are not toys, when your puppy is older, that "playful biting" is going to be a lot more painful.

Dogs are pack animals, descended from wolves, they need a strong leader to feel secure and confident. If they do not have a leader telling them what is or is not correct behavior, puppies can become nervous, anxious, and suffer from separation anxiety. Training is not about being mean or disciplining your puppy, it is about teaching appropriate behavior. Wolf puppies in the wild learn from the pack what is or is not acceptable; many times these "lessons" are in the form of wolf "fights", nips, barks, and pawing from a senior pack member to a wolf puppy. Since your puppy does not have other members of a pack to teach him how to behave, it is your job to provide that structure.

This book is going to teach you to understand the point of view of your puppy, effective training by taking that point of view into consideration, a step-by-step guide to proper training methods, and how to live in harmony with your puppy for years to come. This guide is broken down into seven days, each day's training building on the training from before. Important topics we will cover include: potty training, chewing, crate training, barking, nipping and biting, aggressive behavior, and creating a foundational bond of mutual respect and understanding between you and your puppy.

Day 1: Establishing Your Relationship

As previously discussed, your puppy is a descendant of wolves, and still greatly depends on the instincts that are traditionally attributed to wolves. Understanding wolves may help you better understand your puppy. Wolves hunt in packs, move in packs, sleep in packs, and look to an alpha leader to guide them through life, teaching them what's right and wrong. When any of the wolves do not obey the leader of the pack, that wolf will be disciplined by being placed on their back and a firm grip on their throat by the leader. By placing the disobedient wolf in this position, with his belly in the area, the leader has forced the wolf to obey and submit.

However, wolves and dogs are not exactly wired the same. Dogs were bred from wolves in order to be subordinate and obey, wolves tend to be more cooperative with each other. Even though wolves have a pack leader, the leaders and subordinates work together towards a common goal. Dogs, on the other hand, look to humans for orders and do not work together for a common goal, but together to serve the human. They were bred this way for generations to achieve obedience and dependency on humans.

A recent study conducted at the Oregon State University wanted to test whether dogs were independent problem solvers. Twenty dogs were placed in a room one at a time with a sealed plastic Tupperware container filled with sausage. The goal was to have the dogs figure out how to open the Tupperware container and get the sausage. None of the dogs were able to open the container, and many did not even try. The researchers then let 10 wolves, one at a time, enter the room with the plastic container. Eight out of ten wolves were able to open the container in less than two minutes. When the dogs were led back into the room with the container of sausage along with their owners, they were able to open the containers when directed by their owners to complete the task.

Puppies have been bred to be subordinate and look to their owners for direction. If your puppy is barking, he is looking to you to decide if that is ok; if you yell at your dog, or try to calm him by saying, "It's ok puppy, you're ok," you are actually telling your puppy to continue to bark. Dog's do not understand words, they understand tone and pitch. Sweetly calming your dog, is actually translated to "You're doing a great job, good boy." Yelling at your dog is translated to "Keep going, we are under attack, good boy!" Instead, giving a firm, quick "Ay!" without eye contact, or using a spray bottle, will deliver quick negative reinforcement without using words.

Understanding how your puppy thinks and reacts to training is going to be very helpful for both of you to be successful. You are not being mean by disciplining your puppy, you are guiding your puppy and teaching him appropriate puppy behavior he would have learned from his mother. This is your job now; training begins by understanding that firm, non-emotional queues are the foundation of your corrections and discipline.

Reinforcing your place in the hierarchy and your puppy's subordinate role doesn't mean you don't love your puppy, it means you are his leader, someone he looks up to in order to learn how to operate in the world. We instill these values and concepts in children when they are growing up, it is important to instill these behaviors in your puppy as well in order to create a harmonious and respectful relationship.

The only way you will be able to be successful in training is to understand how your puppy is going to learn best. If you are a visual learner, you are not going to learn well by someone lecturing you. This is the same for puppies, if you do not make yourself the leader, your puppy is going to be nervous, anxious, fearful, and will not be easy to train. By establishing this relationship from day one, you will be leaps ahead in your training by the end of this first week.

Your relationship as leader needs to start on the first day. Until you progress each day through the book, the best concepts to keep in the back of your mind are consistency and repetition. Even though you have not read the chapter on deterring barking, you know that is a boundary. What every training technique shares in common is the basic premise of stopping the behavior and rewarding your puppy when he stops. When you understand this, and accept you are the leader and not being cruel, it will make training a lot easier.

Homework for Day 1: Do a little bit of research on your puppy's specific breed and figure out if that particular breed learns in a specific kind of way. Does your puppy do better early in the morning, or after a long play session? Is your puppy going to respond better to treats or verbal praise only? Consider these possibilities and decide how you are going to reward your puppy and set aside time each day for training.

Day 2: Beginning Potty Training

Starting your training right away is very important in establishing your place in the hierarchy. Your puppy is still a puppy though, so don't be discouraged if your puppy doesn't do everything perfectly the first time. Your home is comforting to you, but it is a completely new environment for your puppy. You can let your puppy settle in up to a week before starting formal puppy training, for example agility training, or sit/stay commands, however you should not delay when training your puppy to cease bad habits, like chewing, biting, barking, and wetting in the house.

Puppies are not able to control the muscles that hold urine in their body until they are about 12 weeks old. So, until your puppy is old enough, remember to offer him plenty of opportunities to go potty outside, usually every 2-3 hours, and yes this includes night time as well. Potty training puppies is hard; it takes a lot of discipline, repetition, and sleeplessness, but it will only last for a short while. Pretty soon you will be thankful you kept at the routine.

Puppies learn from their mothers the appropriate way to relieve themselves. When puppies are first born, they urinate and poop in the kennel or bed they were born in, typically right next to their mother. Sometimes, this area is called the "den". The mothers clean up the puppies' messes to keep the area clean, but as the puppies get older, mother dog starts to nudge her puppies farther and farther away from the den, encouraging the puppies to relieve themselves away from their sleeping and eating area. You have to understand that you are now the mother. You will be the one teaching your puppy where it is appropriate to go potty, and where it is not appropriate.

You should be accompanying your puppy everywhere he goes in the house, so that when you do catch him relieving himself on the floor or carpet, you can stop him midway and immediately place him outside. You do not want to discipline your puppy, or place your puppy outside to go to potty if more than 20 seconds has passed since your puppy relieved himself on the floor. This will confuse your puppy. If you are with your puppy all the time, the moment you see your puppy looking for a place to potty and begin, immediately pick him up (do not yell at your puppy) and put him outside and say "Go potty". Remember, you are acting as his mother, his mother would not shame him when he has an accident, she would calmly correct and redirect.

Setting a timer is helpful, that way you remember to let your puppy out to go potty regularly. Praise your puppy when he walks outside and urinates or poops. If you take your puppy outside to go potty, make sure you keep him focused; do not let him play, run around, or lay down until he has relieved himself. Keep him on track by saying "Go potty" when he gets distracted.

Set your puppy up for success. You do not want to feed your puppy and let him drink water right before bed time and then get upset when he doesn't make it through the night without urinating and pooping. Feed your puppy a few hours before bedtime and pick up the water 3 hours prior to going to sleep. After you feed your puppy, allow him to digest for around 20 minutes and then take him outside. Make sure he goes poop and urinates before you let him back inside.

Most dogs do best when you make a certain area of your yard the place he can relieve himself, making the rest of the yard his play area. Dogs are clean creatures and, just like humans, like to relieve themselves far away from where they eat, play, and sleep. Fencing in a small area, no more than 3' x 3', reinforces that this is where your puppy should go potty. When an area smells like urine, it encourages your puppy to continue urinating there, and communicates that this area is the appropriate place to urinate and defecate.

Homework for Day 2: This is the crucial area to really get started on early because it can be the most destructive behavior. Remember every two to three hours take puppy out to relieve himself, stay with your puppy at all times while he is learning, immediately correct your puppy without yelling or anger, redirect your puppy outside, guide your puppy to the specified area to relieve himself, and keep him focused until he does. Do not forget to praise your puppy when he does a good job; scratches behind the ears, a small treat, or pets are perfect ways in addition to voicing your puppy's good work.

Day 3: Puppy Communication

Puppies have their own language that is essential to understand when beginning training. Everything you do is dependent on your ability to successfully communicate with your puppy. Understanding your puppy's communication style is also going to help you when you start socializing him. At the end of this chapter you will be able to read when your puppy is scared, threatened, aggressive, calm, happy, playful, attentive, and how to correct inappropriate responses to fear. The worst thing you can do when your puppy is scared and reacts aggressively is yell at them. Most individuals adopt older puppies (older than 3-4 months) from shelters these days, many without information on their background or where they lived prior to the shelter. As a result, poor socialization and fear is often seen, but this does not necessarily translate into aggression.

Fear can come in many different forms, from being fearful of different objects, noises, or actions, to being fearful of particular kinds of people like children or men. Quality of life for a fearful dog is low, and can be anxiety provoking for your dog and you. There are four ways dogs react when they are feeling fearful. First, dogs will flea and try to get away from whatever is causing their fear as soon as possible. Another potential reaction is for a dog to freeze and become motionless, like a statute. Your dog could also display a reaction to fear with intense behavior such as

21

excessive water drinking, sniffing, scratching, panting, or eating. Lastly, your dog's reaction to fear could result in aggression. Many owners have a hard time understanding that a dog's aggressive reaction is out of fear, and not because the dog wants to attack or purposefully be aggressive. Your dog is reacting to a perceived threat, the purpose of the aggressive behavior is not to attack, it is to increase the distance between the object or person that is threatening and the dog.

Your dog's body language will tell you a lot about how they are feeling. Although most puppies do not suffer with feelings of fear, chances are your puppy will experience a fearful experience in life. Learning to read your puppy and helping them to respond to stimuli correctly will keep fearful situations later in life from resulting in a fear reaction. If you do not socialize your puppy early by exposing him to many different people and places, your puppy will grow into a fearful dog that, when in an unfamiliar situation, could react aggressively due to his fear.

Fearful body language can be illustrated many different ways, including a body stance that is low to the ground, crouching or laying with their belly turned up to the sky, tail tucked, quick frantic tail wagging, lowered head, large protruding eyes with the white of the eyes showing, ears flattened against your dog's head, a snarl or lips slightly pulled back, and hair between their shoulder blades standing straight up.

The causes of fear can be typically be explained by one of the following three basic reasons.

First, dogs are fearful because of their breed, or genetics, predisposes them to feel fearful. These dogs have less tolerance for stressful or anxiety provoking situations, and breeding these dogs can produce offspring that react similarly.

Secondly, and the most common, is fear caused by lack of proper socialization. As previously noted, exposing your puppy to different people and environments creates confidence. As discussed in a later chapter, socialization should be positive, and never forced. As your puppy develops ways to cope with different situations, he will be able to utilize these tools when he is older. However, socialization does not stop after a few months, socialization should be continued throughout your dog's life.

The third cause of fearful reactions is due to an event that happened in the dog's life that created fear, such as abuse, neglect, or a previous negative experience. For example, a dog might be fearful of other large brown dogs because they were previously attacked by a large brown dog. A dog may have been chased and teased by children, and is now fearful around them. Whatever the experience was, the root cause is a negative situation involving a specific object, environment, or person that the dog is now afraid of.

The most effective method you can employ to prevent fearful behavior with your new puppy is through socialization. Once your puppy is vaccinated, take them regularly for walks, to dog parks, stores that allow you to bring your dog inside, and have friends and family over to meet your new puppy, making sure your puppy is properly handled. If you are already noticing fearful behavior with your puppy the best thing to start with is regular exercise, at least an hour a day in the beginning; exercise supports brain development and mental health for your puppy.

Make sure to start with boundaries when you bring your puppy home. Discuss as a family where you want your puppy to sleep, if he is allowed on couches or beds, not to chase your cats or other animals, not to chew (covered in a later section), etc. You must be calm, but firm, and remember to not yell or react in anger. Consistency, much like it is for children, is reassuring for puppies. Consistency allows the puppies to predict future action from you. When your puppy can predict future actions, this calms any kind of anxiety. Not keeping to your boundaries will cause a fearful and anxious dog.

Even if your dog is not fearful at first, formal training as well as agility training creates happy and well adjusted dogs. Dogs want to be led, and they want their owners to lead them. This builds trust and creates a bond between you and your dog, which further supports your dog's confidence. If you do decide to seek formal training for your dog, make sure the teacher of the class uses "Operant Conditioning", also known as positive reinforcement, as the teaching method. This has consistently been demonstrated as being superior to other training methods.

Other kinds of body language to practice looking for include:

- Tail wagging:
  - regular calm wagging means your puppy is happy
  - exaggerated tail wagging can mean submission
  - slow and stiff wagging usually means anger
  - the tail tucked low over the hips means fear
  - slightly dropped stiff wag can mean anxious
  - generally, a tail that is more than 45 degrees from the back of the dog means friendly and alert.
- Your puppy's ears:
  - pricked up ears means alert and listening
  - flattened ears can mean nervousness or pleasure, it means pleasure when your puppy's eyes are half open, displeasure when your puppy's eyes are big and wide.
- Eye contact:

- o frequent eye contact creates a bond between you and your puppy, but prolonged staring is a threat. Dogs in the wild stare straight into each other's eyes until one backs down or challenges, so do not outstare your puppy.
- Smiles:
  - o Some dogs actually smile! A smile will look like a slightly open mouth mouth with lopsided jaw, that almost looks like your dog is grinning up at you. He is trying to communicate amusement.
  - o When your puppy draws his lips back tightly and teeth are seen, this is fear and aggression.
- Playful Puppy:
  - o When your puppy wants to play he will paw at you, or something around you, or bow down with hips in the air and chest on the ground.
  - o Sometimes your puppy will bark to get your attention, which usually means he wants to play!
- Your Body Language:
  - o Always crouch down and open your arms wide open to signal to your dog you are happy to see them.
  - o Never stand tall, leaning over your dog and stare into their eyes.

Homework for Day 3: Take your puppy to the park, a local coffee shop, or on a walk in a heavily populated area. Start to build up your puppy's confidence. Invite some friends over to visit with your new puppy. Try inviting friends that have children. If you have children come over make sure you are supervising the entire time, teaching the children how to handle a puppy properly (calmly, gently, and with both hands usually sitting on the ground) and teaching your puppy about new kinds of people!

Day 4: Chewing

Little puppies come with very sharp teeth! They do
not know how to control their need to chew and are
probably going to be teething for a long time. Puppies
teeth just like babies; they are going to loose their
teeth and new ones will fill their place. Puppies'
mouths are also the way they explore their world,
figuring out what different objects are in their
environment. Having ample toys for your puppy to
chew on is essential and necessary.

When your puppy is around four to six months of age,
their adult teeth will be growing in and their puppy
teeth will fall out. Their gums are very sensitive
during this time and chewing helps to sooth their
gums. There are several solutions you can use in
order to stop your puppy from inappropriate chewing
while also receiving the relief they need while they are
teething.

It is very important to make sure your puppy does not
have any medical problems contributing to the
chewing. It is not uncommon for many adopted
puppies to come from difficult backgrounds and have
nutritional deficiencies due to poor diet, neglect, or
intestinal parasites that will lead to a disorder called
"pica". Intestinal issues can cause stomach
discomfort which can result in chewing as a way to
cope with the discomfort. Rule out any of these

causes prior to discipline with a thorough check up when you first bring your puppy home.

Puppy proofing your home is going to be very helpful in making sure you set your puppy up for success. Start by looking around your home, what objects look appealing to your new puppy? Any kind of small objects lying around should be picked up, as well as children's toys, shoes, socks, and anything else that might be of interest to your puppy. Tie up electrical cords and place out of your puppy's reach. Household cleaners, chemicals, and any toxic plants should be stored in cabinets and out of your puppy's reach. Any room that is not puppy-proofed should be made inaccessible to your puppy by keeping the doors closed or using baby gates to block the way into the room. We will discuss later about crate training, but that is a great option when you cannot supervise your puppy at all times.

It is important to have plenty of puppy toys around in order to encourage appropriate chewing. The point of this section is not to train your puppy not to chew, it is to train your puppy not to chew the *wrong things*. You want to try a variety of different chew toys because each dog prefers different chew toys and treats. Caution is advised when giving your dog rawhide and beef bones; if you have an intense and determined chewer with strong jaw strength, the rawhide or bone can be whittled down to very small pieces that can then get lodged in their throats. If you do give your puppy a rawhide or beef bone you should supervise your puppy at all times. Never give chicken bones because they are hollow and will splinter, resulting in sharp fragments that can potentially puncture your puppy's fragile digestive system. Many chewing products will help you decide what size is best for your dog; your dog should be able to pick up the toy and carry it around, but it should not be small enough for him to swallow. One of the most common mistakes is to give your dog a chew toy that resembles an object that you do not want your puppy chewing. For example, do not buy a stuffed shoe toy for your puppy, he will not be able to tell the difference between the chew toy and a regular shoe.

I'm sure you are wondering, "but what if I catch my puppy chewing something he shouldn't?" First of all, by puppy-proofing your house, you have made the possibility of chewing minimal, but it's inevitable that your puppy will find something to chew on that they shouldn't! When you see your dog chewing on an inappropriate object, calmly take the object away while saying a short, but firm "no" and then redirecting his attention to his chew toy. When he grabs the chew toy and starts using it, praise him for chewing on the correct object. The key part of this section is repetition, do not let your puppy get away with one session of chewing that he shouldn't, continue to correct calmly and firmly. There are also products you can apply to objects to deter chewing that taste terrible to dogs. The most common is called "bitter apple", and the taste typically keeps dogs away because of the horrible taste.

Lastly, it is important to keep your puppy stimulated everyday. The less stimulation your puppy receives, the more destructive your puppy can get; chewing can often be a coping mechanism for boredom. Providing regular exercise for your puppy also tires him out, a tired puppy is a happy puppy, and he probably won't have the energy to chew.

Homework for Day 4: Chewing can be overcome with these simple steps. First, look around your home and see what needs to be picked up and what rooms need to be closed off to your puppy. Then, go out to your local pet store and purchase several different kinds of chew toys and puppy gates. Bring them home and try them out with your puppy. See which one he likes or which ones he is not interested in. Install your puppy gates to make sure he stays in his puppy proofed area. Don't forget to praise your puppy when he chews on his appropriate chew toys.

Day 5: Barking

Dogs often bark because they are lonely or bored, they will also bark out of fear and wanting to protect their owner. Hopefully, your puppy is not barking out of fear or boredom, which is sometimes harder to control; your puppy is probably barking out of excitement or curiosity. It is impossible to train your puppy never to bark, much like it is impossible to train your puppy never to chew. You want to train your puppy to bark appropriately and to stop when you tell him to stop.

It can be very confusing for puppies when you are inconsistent, as previously mentioned. Consistency is key to a good owner-dog relationship. Responding to barking needs to be consistent no matter what the situation is surrounding the reason your puppy is barking. Many times owners respond differently to their puppy's bark, by either ignoring the bark, yelling at your puppy to stop barking, or encouraging your dog to bark because of a strange noise. This is not helping your puppy to understand appropriate barking, this is just confusing your furry companion that much more.

When your puppy barks, you need to respond consistently each time. After two or three barks, state firmly "Stop Barking", have a treat handy and after saying this, show your puppy the treat and let him smell it. Require your puppy to not bark for three seconds, and then give him the treat. If your puppy continues to bark, repeat the exercise, state firmly "Stop Barking" and hold the treat so your puppy can see. This time make your puppy stop barking for five seconds. Continue to repeat until your puppy successfully settles down and stops barking. Each time you repeat the process, increase the time you are requiring your puppy to stop barking, from five seconds to 10 seconds, to thirty seconds, to up to two minutes if needed.

The purpose of the treat is to focus your puppy to stop barking. Showing your puppy the treat will make your puppy want to close his mouth and prepare for the treat. Once he is chewing, it is difficult to bark and chew at the same time. The most important step in all of this is to stop the barking after two to three barks however you can; you can use a can filled with pennies to shock your puppy to stop barking, a spray bottle works as well. The point is to shock your puppy out of barking, to stop the sound when you say to stop.

The second your puppy stops barking you must immediately praise him and reinforce the good behavior. You can do this with treats, or a "good boy!".

The sequence of events should look like this:
- puppy starts barking
- you let puppy bark two or three times

- you say "Stop barking" while using a spray bottle or removing a treat for your puppy to see,
- as soon as he stops barking, praise your puppy while he is quiet for three seconds (praise during the entire three seconds)
- give your puppy his treat.

Homework for Day 5: Barking is a natural part of a dog's biology, but that doesn't mean it cannot be controlled. Decide whether you want to use a can full of pennies, a spray bottle, or treats to stop your puppy from barking. Once you decide how you are going to stop your puppy from barking, make sure you also purchase treats. Try several different kinds of treats to find out which one your puppy prefers, make sure to try both hard and soft treats. Then start practicing!

Day 6: Mouthing/Biting

Puppies use their mouths to play, this is a very common characteristic and can be very cute when your puppy is 7 or 8 weeks old. But as your puppy grows bigger, suddenly using their mouth to play can hurt! A puppy's mouth is the way it explores his surroundings, how he plays with other puppies, and plays with objects and toys. Puppies with siblings around to play with, will quickly learn that biting to play is not acceptable. Puppies teach each other how to play, and how not to play, typically through the use of "bite inhibition" discussed later. However, if you have a single puppy and he bites you, you cannot turn around and growl or bite back harder (which is what siblings do). You job is to teach your puppy that play biting, or mouthing, is not acceptable play behavior.

First, you can start out by teaching your puppy to be gentle when play biting, this is called "bite inhibition". A puppy that does not understand bite inhibition means that they do not understand the force behind their bite, or their jaw strength. Several well-known dog trainers and behaviorists believe that teaching a puppy or dog bite inhibition will cause the dog to bite less and will be less likely to break skin if he does bite when in a situation of pain or fear.

Bite inhibition is what puppies learn from their siblings when they play together. What happens is that one puppy bites the other puppy too hard during playtime, resulting in a high pitched yelp and playing ceases. The puppy that bit stops playing too because he is shocked and surprised by what the other puppy did; playing will resume, however the puppy that bit too hard will understand that he has to be gentle in order for playing to continue, if he doesn't, then playing will stop.

Since you do not have other puppies to teach your puppy bite inhibition, it is up to you to teach him this important tool. Once you have mastered the bite inhibition, you can move on to teach your puppy not to use his mouth at all during play. However, it is important for your puppy to learn bite inhibition before learning not to use their mouths at all to play, because if for some reason your puppy becomes scared or nervous, you want to have taught your puppy not to bite hard if they must bite at all.

To teach bite inhibition, play with your puppy using your hands, as soon as your puppy bites down hard, immediately yelp, make sure your puppy stops biting, and remove your hands for 10-20 seconds. Then resume playing, and again yelp, wait for your puppy to stop biting, and remove your hands when your puppy bites down too hard. You can repeat this process, making sure not to yelp more than three times in a 15-minute period. If yelping doesn't work to make your puppy stop biting, you can use the words "Too bad" or "Too rough" to startle your puppy. It is important your puppy learns to stop on his own when startled, do not just immediately remove your hands from your puppy's mouth.

Once your puppy stops biting down hard, you can start to yelp when your puppy moderately bites down on your hand, repeating the training sequence above. Eventually you want to train your puppy to play so that you feel little to no pressure at all from his mouth.

The next step is to teach your puppy that human skin is not a play toy. You begin by using a toy or chew bone when your puppy begins to play with your hands. Place the toy in your puppy's mouth and praise him. If your puppy gets excited and tries to mouth you when being pet or stroked, feed your puppy treats from your opposite hand so that your puppy gets used to being touched and stroked without mouthing. You want to emphasize types of play that do not involve your body or hands, for example do not wrestle with your puppy or rough play with your hands. Fetch and tug-of-war are great non-contact ways to play with your puppy, and stimulate him at the same time. If your puppy starts to mouth you, immediately give him a toy and start to play!

If your puppy is a herding breed, he may bite at your feet or ankles. If this is the case, stop walking immediately when your puppy starts biting, and hand him a toy. If you do not have a toy with you, stop walking and as soon as your puppy stops biting, praise him and go get him a toy. Make sure to keep a wide variety of toys around so your puppy does not become bored, and has plenty of objects to chew on.

Homework for Day 6: It is time to begin teaching your puppy bite inhibition. Try the training sequence outlined above, playing with your puppy using your hands and yelping when your puppy bites down hard. Remember not to let your puppy bite down hard more than three times in a 15-minute period. You can resume once the 15 minutes is up, and begin again, repeating this sequence 2-3 times. Try to practice this everyday, until you no longer feel pressure, or only slight pressure, when your hand is in your puppy's mouth.

Day 7: Crate Training

Crate training is especially helpful when you first bring your new puppy home. A crate can serve as a safe space for your puppy to relax, useful potty training technique, safe way to transport your puppy, and helpful when you need to leave the house and your puppy is still learning appropriate behavior. Crate training is incredibly successful, however if you do not do it correctly, you can end up teaching your dog to be fearful of his crate. A puppy should never be forced into a crate; he should always walk in of his own free will.

First, you want to casually introduce the crate into the home as if it is just another piece of furniture. Do not bring the crate home and immediately place your puppy inside and lock the door. Next, place the crate somewhere in the house that your puppy frequently spends time in, such as next to your bed, in the living room, or an office. Place a blanket and a few of your puppy's toys in the crate and keep the door open. Some puppies will immediately start sniffing the crate and exploring, however if your puppy is hesitant, start by placing your puppy's food and favorite toys near and inside the crate. You want to have your puppy be comfortable with walking inside the crate by himself. Be patient, it can take days for this to happen, so just keep calmly introducing your puppy to the crate until he is able to comfortably walk inside.

The next goal is to have your puppy feel comfortable about staying in the crate for long periods of time, with the door open. A popular and successful way of doing this is to feed your puppy each time inside the crate. Place the food at the back of the crate so that your puppy's entire body is inside. If your puppy is not willing to put his entire body in the crate yet for extended periods of time, start by placing the food just on the inside, close to the opening. Slowly move the food dish further and further back, until your puppy successfully eats while fully inside the crate.

Once your puppy is eating his entire meal while standing completely inside the crate, you are ready to try closing the door. First, place the food in your puppy's crate, as soon as your puppy is inside his crate, close the door. As soon as your puppy finishes eating, immediately open the door and allow your puppy to exit. Each time you will leave the door closed for longer periods of time. If your puppy starts whining, let your puppy out immediately, you do not want to teach your dog that his crate is something to fear. Next time, if your puppy whines again, only open the door once he stops whining because you do not want to teach him that whining means to open the door.

Once your puppy is able to stay in his crate for extended periods of time during his meal time, it is time to try leaving your puppy in his crate for an extended period of time not during a meal time. Lead your puppy into the crate using a favorite toy or a treat. Close the door behind your puppy and walk into another room for a few minutes. When you return, sit down next to the cage for a few minutes and then open the door. Do not come back into the room and immediately open the crate door. Keep increasing the time until you are able to leave the room for 30 minutes without your puppy becoming stressed. Once your puppy is able to stay comfortably in the crate for 30 minutes, it is time to try letting your puppy sleep overnight in the crate, remembering to let your puppy out for potty breaks.

Eventually you can leave your puppy in his crate when you leave the house. Remember to act calm and avoid any kind of excitement. Crate training should be viewed as completely normal to your puppy, some puppies really enjoy their quiet time to themselves in their crates. Calmly leave the house, and when you return remain very calm and do not excite your puppy. You want to ignore any kind of excited behavior from your puppy. Once your puppy is settled, and no longer showing excitement, you can greet your puppy calmly.

Crate training is also great for puppies that suffer from separation anxiety. Their crate becomes their safe place when they have to separate from you, providing a comfortable and quiet den. It may be a little more challenging to crate train your puppy if he is prone to separation anxiety, but remember to be patient and persistent. Keep trying each step everyday, you may simply move slower through the steps, but you will succeed. Dogs are den animals and receive comfort in enclosed comfortable places.

Homework for Day 7: Purchase your crate! Your crate should be big enough for your puppy to stand up all the way and turn around comfortably. You want it small enough to create a feeling of a den, while making sure your puppy can move around comfortably. You can take your puppy to the store with you and have a sales person help you decide on the right size. Remember, your puppy is going to eventually grow bigger, so you will have to buy a bigger crate when they are older.

Conclusion

The bond between a dog and his owner is unlike many of the other bonds people experience in everyday life. Creating a healthy and strong bond is essential to a happy and well adjusted dog, as well as a stress-free life for you. A fearful and uncomfortable dog can effect your day to day life. Walking your dog around the block can turn into a struggle and taking your dog on trips can turn into a constant barking session. In order to enjoy your relationship, training is essential.

Your puppy is going to look to you to be his leader, if you do not take up that role, your relationship will be strained, and you and your puppy will continue to struggle with each other. It is natural to be your puppy's leader, so embrace it!

I hope you have enjoyed learning about creating a happy relationship between you and your puppy using the simple day-by-day training sequences described in this book. Thank you for reading this book and please leave a review if you enjoyed it so others can enjoy it as well!

19159080R00032

Printed in Great Britain
by Amazon